Paul
and friends

Story by Penny Frank
Illustrated by Eric Ford

THE LION
STORY BIBLE

51

OXFORD · BATAVIA · SYDNEY

C
E
Pen

The Bible tells us
how God sent his Son Jesus to show
us what God is like and how we can
belong to God's kingdom.
This story is about some of the
adventures of a man called Paul. He
had been a leader of the Jews, who
tried to stop the followers of Jesus
telling others about him. Paul put
many of them into prison.
But then he saw Jesus for himself
and became his follower.
You can find this story in your
own Bible, in the book of Acts.

Copyright © 1987 Lion Publishing

Published by
Lion Publishing plc
Sandy Lane West, Littlemore, Oxford, England
ISBN 0 85648 776 7
ISBN 0 7459 1796 8 (paperback)
Lion Publishing Corporation
1705 Hubbard Avenue, Batavia, Illinois 60510, USA
ISBN 0 85648 776 7
Albatross Books Pty Ltd
PO Box 320, Sutherland, NSW 2232, Australia
ISBN 0 86760 561 8
ISBN 0 7324 0116 X (paperback)

First edition 1987, reprinted 1987, 1988
Paperback edition 1989

British Library Cataloguing in Publication Data

Frank, Penny
Paul and friends. – (The Lion Story Bible; 51)
1. Paul, *the Apostle, Saint* – Juvenile literature
I. Title   II. Ford, Eric
225.9'24   BS2506.S
ISBN 0-85648-776-7
ISBN 0-7459-1796-8 (paperback)

Printed in Yugoslavia

Library of Congress Cataloging in Publication Data

Frank, Penny.
Paul and friends.
(The Lion Story Bible; 51)
1. Paul, the Apostle, Saint – Juvenile literature. 2. Bible. N.T. – Biography – Juvenile literature. 3. Bible stories, English – N.T. Acts. [1. Paul, the Apostle, Saint, 2. Bible stories – N.T.]
I. Ford, Eric, ill. II. Title. III. Series: Frank, Penny. Lion Story Bible; 51.
BS2506.5.F7 1987   226'.609505
86-4703
ISBN 0-85648-776-7
ISBN 0-7459-1796-8 (paperback)

When Paul set out for the city of Damascus, he wanted to arrest anyone who talked about Jesus and to throw them into prison.

But, on the way to Damascus, God stopped him and spoke to him.

Paul ended up by wanting to talk about Jesus himself!

The followers of Jesus in Damascus were very excited.

'Paul is one of us now,' they said. 'He will want to preach about Jesus, instead of throwing us into prison.'

'How can Paul change his mind like that?' Paul's old friends asked each other. 'We must kill him before he starts spreading this story about Jesus coming to life again.'

But the followers of Jesus heard of their plan, and one night they helped Paul to escape from Damascus. They let him down from the city wall in a basket!

In the city of Antioch, followers of Jesus were sharing the good news. The people there were excited.

'We need to be different,' some of them said. 'Can God make us into new people, too?'

So many believed and turned to God,
that the people in Antioch began to call
the followers of Jesus Christ by a new
name. They called them Christians.

News from Antioch reached Jerusalem. A man called Barnabas went to help, and he asked Paul to join him.

They saw that, when people believed in Jesus, God gave each of them a job to do. He gave some of them special power to heal sick people. Some found that they were able to preach. Others had the special job of helping people.

Everyone knew that God had given Paul and Barnabas a very special job. The people of Antioch could not keep them there. They must travel to other towns and cities with the good news of Jesus.

When Paul and Barnabas arrived at Lystra, they started to tell people in the street the good news about Jesus.

One person who listened to every word was a poor, crippled man, who had never been able to walk.

The man believed all that Paul said. Paul knew that God would heal him.

'Stand up,' Paul said.

The man jumped up. He started walking around. His legs became strong and healthy.

When the crowds saw what had
happened, they thought that Paul and
Barnabas had done this by themselves.
   'They must be gods, pretending to be
men,' the people shouted.

'Don't be silly,' Paul said. 'We are just ordinary people, like you. We have come to bring good news from the God who made our world. It is his power that made the lame man walk. You must believe in him.'

After many long journeys, Paul and Barnabas went to Jerusalem. There the leaders were waiting to talk to them. They had an important meeting.

'First of all, we thought that God's good news was just for his special people, the Jews,' said Simon Peter. 'But now we wonder if God wants everyone to hear about it. What do you think, Paul?'

So Paul and Barnabas stood up and told of the adventures they had had. They told them about the people who had been healed and the people God had changed by giving them his Holy Spirit.

'God is doing all this for people everywhere,' said Paul, 'not just for his special people, the Jews. So we know his plan is for the whole world to hear the good news.'

All the apostles and leaders agreed with him.

So Paul set off again with the good
news. This time he took a friend called
Silas. They went by land and sea, until
they came to the city of Philippi.

As soon as they arrived, they went to
a place on the river bank where people
met to pray. Paul told them about Jesus,
and the good news that they could be
forgiven and start a new life.

Many people in Philippi believed what Paul and Silas were teaching. But others made trouble. Paul and Silas were marched off to prison.

The two men were whipped and locked up for the night.

Paul and Silas sat in the dirty, smelly prison. It was very late and their backs hurt badly, where they had been whipped. But they began to pray and to sing songs of praise to God. They sang about his love and power. They sang about Jesus and how he had risen to life again.

While they were singing, the ground shook and the prison walls trembled. It was an earthquake!

The locks on the doors were shaken loose. The prisoners were free!

The prison guard came running in. If the prisoners escaped, he would be killed.

But, to his amazement, Paul called out, 'We are all here.'

'This is the work of your God,' the guard said. 'He has set you free. I want him to forgive me and to be my God too.'

So the prison guard and all his family believed in God and became followers of Jesus.

Paul journeyed on. He knew there were so many people who had never even heard of Jesus.

He wanted to use every moment, telling them God's good news.

The Lion Story Bible is made up of 52 individual stories for young readers, building up an understanding of the Bible as one story — God's story — a story for all time and all people.

The New Testament section (numbers 31–52) covers the life and teaching of God's Son, Jesus. The stories are about the people he met, what he did and what he said. Almost all we know about the life of Jesus is recorded in the four Gospels — Matthew, Mark, Luke and John. The word gospel means 'good news'.

The last four stories in this section are about the first Christians, who started to tell others the 'good news', as Jesus had commanded them — a story which continues today all over the world.

The stories in *Paul and friends* come from the New Testament book of Acts: the Damascus story from chapter 9; the Antioch story from chapters 11 and 13; Lystra from chapter 14; the Jerusalem Council from chapter 15; Philippi from chapter 16.

When Paul first became a Christian, God warned him how much he would suffer for Jesus' sake. But Paul never once turned back. He simply *had* to tell people the good news. He owed it to them. And, although in every place there was opposition, in every place, too, he found some who were eager to listen. More and more decided to follow Jesus.

The letters Paul wrote to help these little groups of Christians form more than one-third of the New Testament. The last book in this series, number 52: *Paul the prisoner*, tells how those letters came to be written, and the story of a shipwreck.